I am Beautiful!

By Jhala Angelique

Illustrations By Keith Butler Jr.

Editor: Angela Kelly

Typesetting: Monica Summer

I would like to dedicate the "I AM.." Series to our Beautiful and Powerful Grandmother, Lola Fay Kelly Woodard. Thank You Great-Grandmother for the legacy of Wisdom. Strength, True Beauty, Love, and Courage, that this bloodline will continue to carry on. As You watch from Heaven we hope to make you proud Grandmother.

To My Contributors: Thank You, To My Amazing Mom, Angela Kelly For All Of The Sacrifices, Abundant Love, Support, and Prayers; Thanks Dad (Ja'Mil Welch) For Your Love & Prayers; Thanks To My Super Supportive Brother: Don, and Sisters: Danielle & Monica Summer;Thanks Auntie Clarice Ligon-Johnson & Auntie Katherine Haslem For Your Encouragement & Support; Special Thanks To Keith Butler Sr For Coming To Our Rescue & Introducing Us To Such An Amazing Artist: Keith Butler Jr.

Thank You God For The Gifts...

IN GOD'S EYES THERE IS NO EMPHASIS ON THE COLOR OF YOUR SKIN (BE IT LIGHT SKINNED, DARK SKINNED, RED SKINNED, YELLOW SKINNED, OR WHITE; THERE ARE NO COLOR LINES). THERE IS, AN EMPHASIS ON THE CONTENT OF OUR HEARTS, THE CONTENT OF OUR CHARACTER, THE USE OF OUR GIFTS AND TALENTS, AND THE ACTIONS OF PEOPLE....(Angela Kelly)

Hello! Did you know that when you look into a mirror that you are beautiful? No matter what color, creed, or shape that you appear, You are beautifully and wonderfully made. Everyone has differences, but it's our differences that makes us unique and special.

Let me tell you a story about an experience that took place while I was attending school. At this particular time, I had started a new school and was very excited about the school year and a new experience.

While most kids are nervous about entering a new school and having to find new friends I was ready for the challenge and a new journey!

The first and second week went well. My teacher was pretty cool and my classmates seemed to like me. I had high hopes for this school year!

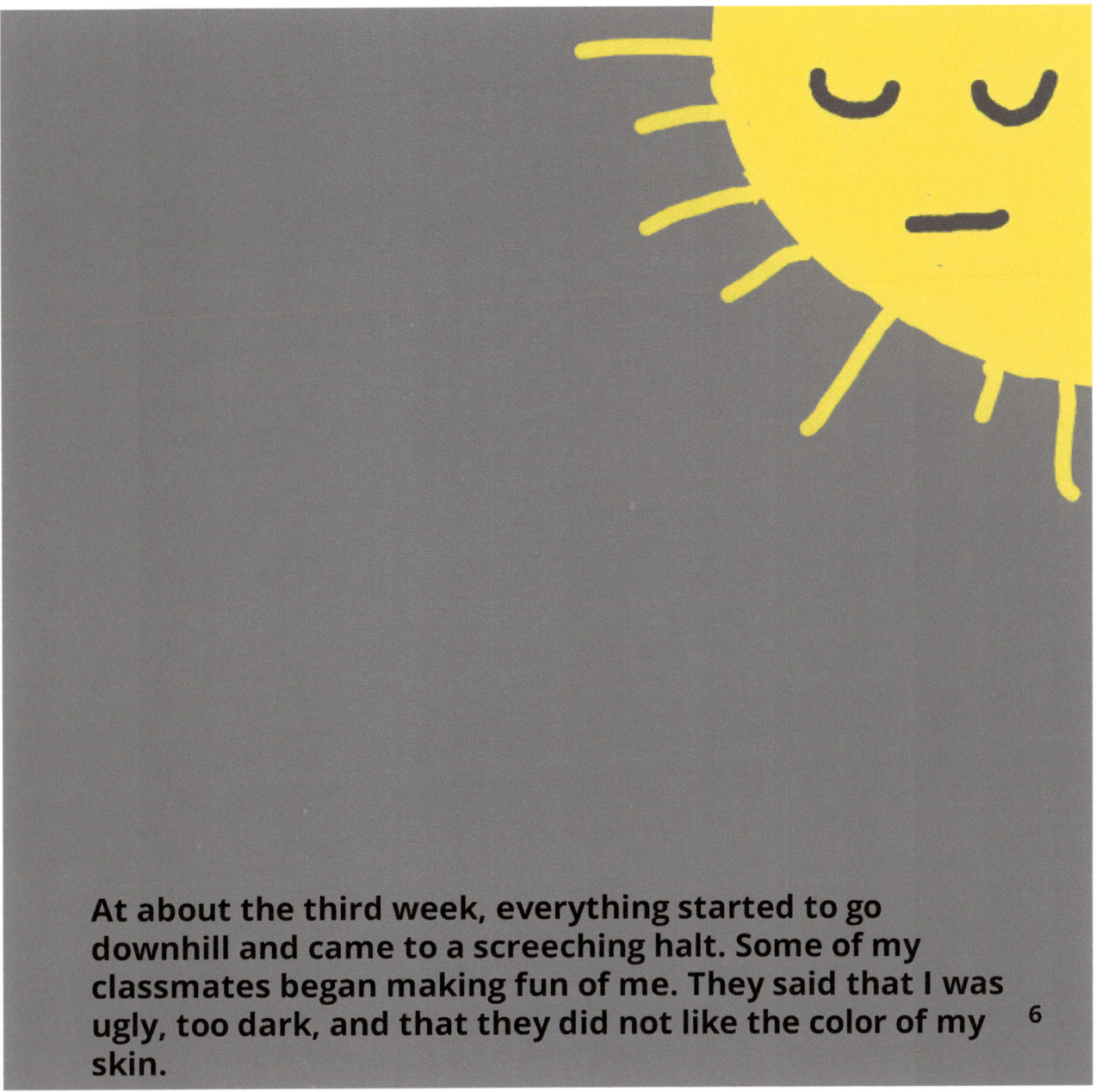

At about the third week, everything started to go downhill and came to a screeching halt. Some of my classmates began making fun of me. They said that I was ugly, too dark, and that they did not like the color of my skin.

In the midst of my hurt and now feelings of insecurity, I could hear my mom's voice reminding me, "That I was beautiful and wonderfully made." While this gave me a boost of positive energy for a short period of time, things soon got worse!

My classmates would run up to me, take turns hitting me in the back, and run away. The few classmates that were brave enough to play with me at first, told me that they could no longer play with me, and didn't. This shaming devastated me even more and I began to feel really alone.

I now found myself not wanting to go to school. I often cried and begged my mom to allow me to stay home.

My Mom didn't know that I was being bullied until she visited my school and witnessed it firsthand. She was not only shocked, but was equally disappointed and upset.

We were often in the principal's office, with hopes of resolving the bullying issues, that I was having with some of my classmates.

After a LONG semester, my mom made the decision to remove me from that school. To be quite honest, I was so relieved! I was so grateful and now I felt safe again!

I thank God that I have a wonderful mother and mentor, who understands the importance of building the self esteem of her children. My mother teaches us that, "Whatever you pour into the pot, is what you will get out". She believes that children are indeed a gift from Heaven. She constantly reminds me of the great work that God did when He created me.

During the time that I was being bullied, all that my parents had taught me, as well as my confidence that was once a crown for me, seemed to have been lost in the pile of negativity and brokenness. I felt fear, disappointment, sadness, anger and loneliness. I no longer believed in myself.

I could not even express what I was feeling to my parents. I later learned how to express myself. I learned that the more that I talked about how I felt with my family, the more I began to feel better about myself. I realized that it is important to talk to my parents, especially since they are our first teachers and protectors.

I now had the confidence that I was wonderfully made, that I was strong, courageous, fierce, gifted, and talented! I now regained my crown! I was able to look in the mirror and not only see the BEAUTIFUL me, but I was now able to SPEAK to the BEAUTIFUL me once again, I am BEAUTIFUL...! Hello BEAUTIFUL! Good morning BEAUTIFUL! Goodnight BEAUTIFUL!

I want to encourage YOU! If you have experienced bullying, and a loss of who YOU are, or don't know that YOU TOO are beautifully and wonderfully made. Look in the mirror and SPEAK to that Handsome, Beautiful, Courageous, Gifted, and Talented person that you see in the mirror.

That was my story. Many of you, may have similar experiences. I decided to share my experience with the hope that you understand that you are not alone. Together we can make a difference in the fight against bullying. How, you might ask?

By telling your parents first, telling your teachers, and any other grownups that will listen, and that you trust.

Second, by understanding who you are and the power that you have. Third, By exposing the bullies... YOU ARE NOT ALONE!!!!

Just believe in yourself and believe in the power that you have inside of you!

$12.50
ISBN 978-1-7338202-1-9

9 781733 820219

51250>

www.ingramcontent.com/pod-product-compliance
Lightning Source LLC
Chambersburg PA
CBHW041544040426

42446CB00003B/229